BRITAIN PORTRAYED

BRITAIN PORTRAYED

A REGENCY ALBUM 1780–1830

JOHN BARR

The British Library

© 1989 The British Library Board
First Published 1989 by The British Library, Great Russell Street, London WC1B 3DG.

British Library Cataloguing in Publication Data

British Library
    Britain portrayed : a Regency album, 1780–1830.
    1. Aquatints: Special subjects. Great Britain, history
    I. Title   II. Barr, John, *1934–*
    769'.4941073

    ISBN 0–7123–0174–7

Designed by Roger Davies. Typeset by Bexhill Phototypesetters, Bexhill-on-Sea, E. Sussex. Colour reproduction by York House Graphics, Hanwell, Middlesex. Printed in Italy by Motta.

Photographs by Chris Lee, British Library Photographic Service.
Figs 13 and 14 are reproduced by courtesy of the Trustees of the British Museum.

A

PICTURESQUE TOUR

OF

THE ENGLISH LAKES,

CONTAINING A

DESCRIPTION OF THE MOST ROMANTIC SCENERY

OF

Cumberland, Westmoreland, and Lancashire,

WITH

ACCOUNTS OF ANTIENT AND MODERN MANNERS AND CUSTOMS,

AND ELUCIDATIONS OF

THE HISTORY AND ANTIQUITIES

OF THAT PART OF THE COUNTRY, &c. &c.

ILLUSTRATED WITH

FORTY-EIGHT COLOURED VIEWS,

DRAWN BY MESSRS. T. H. FIELDING, AND J. WALTON,

DURING A TWO YEARS RESIDENCE AMONG THE LAKES.

LONDON:
PRINTED FOR R. ACKERMANN, 101, STRAND.

MDCCCXXI.

Contents

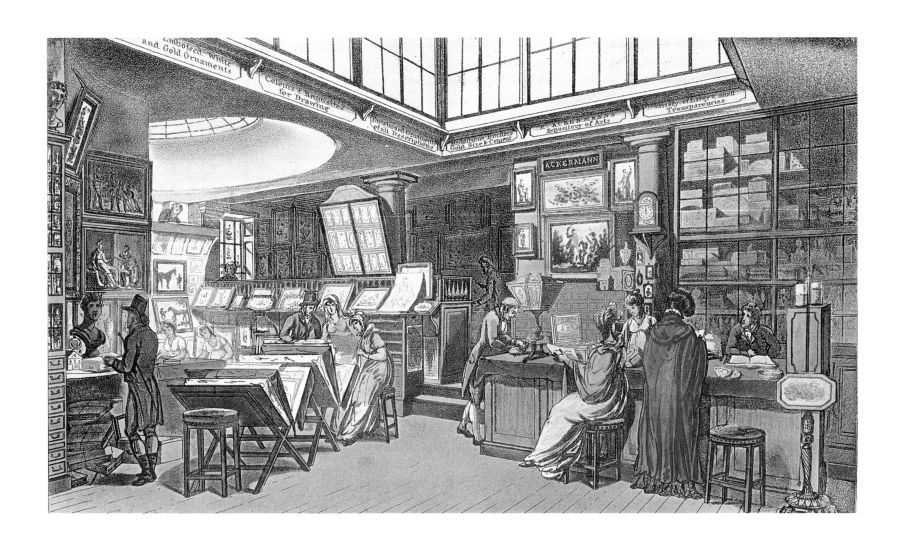

Introduction

THIS BOOK is an album showing something of the life and landscape of Britain as recorded in aquatint by artists working around 1800. These artists created peep-holes, as it were, through which we can view the past. We see their surroundings and way of life as they saw them, or perhaps as their patrons, publishers and customers wished to see them.

The illustrations are arranged here to form an armchair tour of Britain, with brief explanations of their subjects, drawing where possible on the guide-books and other descriptions produced at the time. 'Old guide-books, so out-of-date as to be historical documents, make excellent travelling companions', considered Aldous Huxley, (*Along the Road*, 1925). One can easily agree with Huxley that 'it is delightful to read on the spot the impressions and opinions of tourists, who visited . . . in the vehicles and with the aesthetic prejudices of the period, the places you are visiting now. The voyage ceases to be a mere tour through space . . . You travel through time and thought as well. They are morally wholesome reading too, for they make one realise the entirely accidental character of all our tastes'. Or as one such tourist, George Saville Carey, introducing *The Balnea, or an impartial description of all the popular watering-places in England* (1801) wrote: 'The reader often feels as great a satisfaction in going over the excursions of another in print as if he trod the ground himself; at any rate, it is less irksome and less expensive.'

Regency Britain

In the early decades of the nineteenth century the towns, villages and countryside of the British Isles attained a beauty and comeliness unsurpassed before or since, judging by contemporary illustration. Even when we make allowance for the preferences of patrons and

Fig. 1 **Ackermann's Repository of Arts, 101 Strand**

Drawn by T. Rowlandson

From this address in The Strand Ackermann published his illustrated books and *The Repository of Arts, Literature, Commerce, Manufactures, Fashions and Politics*, a 'glossy' magazine in which this illustration appeared.

The Repository of Arts, 1809. 129 × 220 mm. [K.Top.27.16.1]

customers and for some artist's licence, the right conditions apparently prevailed for a visually satisfying balance between the natural and the man-made.

Local building stones and timber had not yet been displaced by rail-freighted brick, slates and iron; concrete and asphalt were then unknown. Slow transport by road, canal or coastal shipping favoured the persistence of vernacular building styles and the survival of regional and occupational costume. Crumbling castles and ivy-clad ruins were left untouched by the hand of restoration and repair, presenting a picture of pleasing decay. On the other hand, the enclosures and planting of trees and hedges had been completed, and the landscaped parks of 'Capability' Brown and Humphry Repton were now reaching maturity.

London, with nearly a million inhabitants, was by far the most populous city in the world and the greatest port. The Thames remained a natural thoroughfare and tradesmen still lived in the City, 'over the shop'. London retained her Wren churches intact and was gaining the stucco palaces, villas and terraces of John Nash. The houses, gardens, furniture and fashions of the rich were admired and imitated throughout Europe and beyond.

In fixing this perfect moment, the artists and publishers of topographical prints were catering in the first place for a revived interest in British scenery and antiquities. Tourists, prevented by war with revolutionary France from travelling on the Continent, were discovering their own country. These prints also promoted and celebrated a mood of national self-confidence and pride in Britain's military and naval victories (*Frontispiece; Plate, p.49; Fig.16*), technical innovations, and agricultural wealth (*Plate, p.81*). National self-esteem was further gratified by representations of the mansions and parks of the nobility and gentry, of sport as a distinctively British pastime, and of the splendour and modernity of the metropolis.

The techniques

The early nineteenth century was the great period of English watercolour, a medium in which artists set down with accuracy and directness their experience of the

FIGS 2.3 **New Palace Yard, Westminster**

Drawn and engraved by Thomas Malton

Malton drew and aquatinted in monochrome a dozen London views, of which this is one. Here are his unsigned watercolour drawing and the aquatint after it (Fig. 3), showing New Palace Yard, a courtyard in front of Westminster Hall – the 'New Palace' of Richard II.

Published 28 May 1782. 420 × 575 mm. [K.Top.22.15.b,c]

landscape, and caught the changing light and weather of a northern, maritime climate.

In hand-coloured aquatint, combined with line etching, the subtle and spontaneous effects of water-colour washes were reproduced in prints that are often almost indistinguishable from the artists' originals. These prints were issued separately or in instalments, and collected in albums; some were published with an ancillary text in colour-plate books.

Colour-plate books are now rare, partly because the plates could only be issued in relatively small print-runs and partly because so many copies have since been broken up to obtain prints for framing. These fade after long exposure to light, but those aquatints surviving in the volumes for which they were made remain as fresh and vivid as ever. This is true of the plates in the British Library's copies of the books and of the prints preserved in the guard-books of the King's Topographical Collection, acquired by the British Museum in 1828 as part of the library of King George III.

The introduction of aquatint

Paul Sandby, a military draughtsman and drawing master, was the first artist to make extensive use of aquatint in this country. He learned the rudiments of the process from the Hon. Charles Greville, who apparently purchased it on the Continent from its inventor, Jean-Baptiste Le Prince. Sandby adapted and improved aquatint 'as a mode for imitating drawings', notably in his collections of monochrome sepia Welsh views published in 1776–77 (*Plate, p.91*). In these he introduced to a wider public the austere and rugged scenery of Wales and to the publishers of topographical prints a new medium, suitable for reproducing watercolour drawings.

The washes of watercolour were imitated in blue-grey (*Figs 2,3*) and light brown inks, and soon two or even three colours were printed from the same plate. The remaining tints were applied by hand.

In England from the 1790s until the 1830s, when steel

FIG. 3 *See* Fig. 2

engraving and lithography began to supplant it, aquatint supplemented by hand-colouring was used to illustrate a well-defined group of subjects: topography, including architecture and gardens (*Fig. 17*), costume and uniforms, and caricature and sport (*Plates, pp.71, 105*). In their colour-plate books Rudolf Ackermann and other publishers raised book illustration in England to a level which has rarely been equalled. The less ambitious prints produced as modest souvenirs of particular occasions show unusual aspects of contemporary life (*Plates, pp.49,61*).

How aquatinting was done

'An aquatint is produced entirely by means of biting with acid', wrote Sarah Prideaux in her pioneering study, 'and is therefore, in the strict sense of the word, etched'. In etching, a copper plate is first coated with a thin ground of wax and lamp-black. The design is drawn in this ground with a metal point, laying bare parts of the copper. The plate is then immersed in acid until the lightest lines have been 'bitten' where the copper has been eaten away. These lines are then 'stopped out' with acid-resisting varnish, and the process repeated until the lines darkest to print have been 'bitten' to the required depth. In stipple, a pointed needle is used to build up a mass of dots on an etching ground in order to provide areas of tone in the resulting print.

Aquatint, like mezzotint, renders areas of tone. Both methods require the roughening of a copper plate from which impressions are taken: in mezzotint by means of a serrated tool called a rocker; and in aquatint by a variant of etching, that is, by the biting of acid into a copper plate which is partially protected by an evenly laid ground of resin particles. The ground is laid on the copper plate, either by settling a cloud of powdered resin dust across it, or by the evaporation of a solution to leave a granular deposit. The particles are then fused to the plate by heat and they resist the biting of the acid. The tiny ring-like depressions bitten around each particle retain the ink and print areas of soft, grainy tone. The lightest tints are printed first and then stopped out with varnish. To obtain variations in tone careful repeats of

FIG. 4 **Dunstanborough Castle**

Drawn by J. M. W. Turner

The engravers made masterly transcriptions on to copper plates of Turner's watercolours for the volumes of *Picturesque views in England and Wales*, helped by Turner's comments on their proof impressions. They received about £100 for each plate from the publisher, while Turner was paid about half that sum.

Picturesque views in England and Wales from drawings of J. M. W. Turner, 1838. vol. I. [746.e.2]

Figs 5,6 **Internal view of Westminster Hall**

Drawn and engraved by G. Hawkins

In the early nineteenth century Westminster Hall, built 1394–97 by Richard II, with its hammer-beam roof spanning 68 feet, was still the largest room unsupported by columns to be found anywhere. It was usually crowded with judges, barristers, witnesses, sightseers, and even stall-holders selling law-books and clothing. Here we see the artist's preliminary pencil drawing and his finished aquatint (Fig. 6).

Published by G. Hawkins, February 1801. 440 × 370 mm.
[K.Top.24.24.k,i]

'stopping out' are needed, together with precise timing in the exposure of the plates to the acid.

In sugar aquatint the plate is covered completely with resinous particles. The artist then paints his design directly on the surface in a mixture of sugar, gouache and water. The whole plate is then completely coated in varnish, and immersed in water, until the sugar swells and lifts the varnish off. Those parts bearing the artist's design are thus exposed and the design is bitten by the acid and printed. This process is positive and has the advantage that the artist can see what the final design will look like.

Since aquatint was a purely tonal effect, the lines, dots and hatching of a design had to be etched or engraved on the plate. Aquatint was generally used in combination with line etching, and sometimes as an ingredient in 'mixed media' prints. In J.M.W. Turner's engraving of Dunstanborough Castle (*Fig. 4*), for example, some amalgamation of aquatint with mezzotint and etching was apparently made by the engraver without the artist's permission; Turner wrote on the proof 'Sir, you have done in aquatint all the castle down to the rocks; did I ever ask for such an indulgence?'

Printing

In printing by any *intaglio* process (aquatint, copper engraving, etching) the copper plate is inked with a pad and the surplus ink wiped off the surface. The ink remaining in the lines or marks below the surface of the plate is transferred by pressure onto the paper. The deepest furrows, holding the most ink, print the darkest. In aquatint, the pits between the granules hold the ink and print areas of tone.

Printing the edition was an exacting process. A soft wove paper, usually that made by Whatman, was dampened and sized to prevent colour seeping through. The plate was first heated to help the ink run into the tiny pits and re-heated before it was placed in the rolling press with the dampened paper. The printer turned the rollers, applying enough pressure to force the paper into the inked depressions. The printed sheet was removed and dried and the plate cleaned for the next print.

FIG. 7 **Crummock Water**

Drawn and aquatinted by William Green

Green's prints form a remarkable record of the mountains, lakes and buildings of the Lake District when there were fewer trees and fewer people to be seen there.

Published by W. Green, Manchester, c.1795. 287 × 451 mm. [K.Top.10.40a]

Publishers understandably would run off only as many impressions as they thought they could sell. Copper plates wear quickly, and this restricted the number of good impressions that can be taken without retouching.

Colour in aquatint

The earliest aquatints were printed in a neutral monochrome, but before long the foundation washes of watercolour were imitated in brown for foreground and blues and greys for sky and distance. Other colours were applied by hand; the hand-colouring of each print took at least as much time as its printing. Printing in two or even three tints from the one plate reduced hand-colouring to a minimum. This was a skilled task in which factories of colourists were employed, sometimes French refugees, often children. The laying of even washes in the correct colour called for sureness of hand and eye. Both Turner and Girtin served apprenticeships in tinting prints. Colouring ranged in quality from close copying of the artist's master drawing to the hurried application of dashes of paint as the print passed from one colourist to another. Hand-colouring added to the expense of publication; some copies of colour-plate books were issued with plain, uncoloured illustrations and sold at a lower price.

The artists, publishers and purchasers

The Picturesque

William Wordsworth in 1844 wrote a letter to the editor of the *Morning Post* protesting against the extension of the railway into the Lake District beyond Kendal. He recalled that 'the relish for choice and picturesque natural scenery (a poor and mean word which requires an apology but will be generally understood) is of quite recent origin'.

'Rocks and mountains, torrents and wide-spread waters, and all those features of nature which . . . this part of England is distinguished for, cannot, in their finer relations to the human mind, be comprehended, or even very perfectly conceived without opportunities of observation in some degree habitual', he continued.

FIG. 8 **A view from the east-end of the Brewery, Chiswell Street**
Mezzotint by W. Ward after a painting by G. Garrard, 'painter of horses to H.R.H. the Prince of Wales'
In 1750 the brewer Samuel Whitbread removed his business to Chiswell Street. John Rennie and other engineers later devised improvements in the brewery, where beer was still brewed as late as 1976. In mezzotint, gradations of tone and chiaroscuro could be rendered which were not possible in aquatint.
Published by G. Garrard and W. Ward, 1792. 435 × 550 mm. [K.Top.27.32.1]

This taste for natural scenery was also something to be learned before it could be gratified. The principal instructor was a clergyman and schoolmaster, the Revd William Gilpin (1724–1804), who largely invented the idea of the picturesque.

Gilpin spent his summer vacations making 'picturesque tours' in various parts of Britain. In his published accounts of them he taught people to look at scenery from the point of view of 'picturesque beauty', which he defined simply as 'that which would look well in a picture'. The pictures he had in mind were those seen and collected by English gentlemen on the Grand Tour, painted in Italy by Claude Lorrain, Salvator Rosa, Gaspard Dughet and other seventeenth-century artists. The tourists on their return from Italy sought to appreciate the landscapes of their native land in terms of such pictures – often with the aid of a 'Claude glass', a darkened, slightly convex mirror, in which the viewer, having turned his back upon a scene, could recompose it to best advantage.

Gilpin described the views he considered worth admiring and told his readers the places from which to look at them. He expounded his theory and its local applications in a series of guide-books illustrated by sepia aquatints after his own indifferent sketches. Gilpin thought that in some instances 'nature is most defective in composition and must be a little assisted'. As he wrote to a friend in 1784, 'I am so attached to my picturesque rules, that if nature gets it wrong, I cannot help putting her right'.

'The horse is in itself certainly a nobler animal than the cow', Gilpin conceded, 'but in a picturesque light the cow has undoubtedly the advantage.' (*Fig. 7.*) 'Roughness forms the most essential part of the difference between the beautiful and the picturesque', he explained. 'A piece of Palladian architecture may be elegant in the last degree (*Plate p.81*) but should we wish to give it picturesque beauty we must use the mallet instead of the chisel; we must beat down one half of it, deface the other and throw the mutilated members around in heaps.' (*Plates, pp.107,113.*) Gilpin eventually provoked the ridicule of William Combe and Thomas Rowlandson in the satirical accounts in verse

FIG. 9 **Glass-houses near Exeter**

Drawn and engraved by J. Hassell

Glass was made in furnaces in glass-houses similar to pottery kilns. John Hassell also published prints showing a tin mine in Cornwall and iron works near Tintern Abbey.

Published 1798. [K.Top.11.69y]

published by Rudolph Ackermann of the tours of Dr Syntax, a sketching pedagogue. Nevertheless Gilpin's prescriptions, though sometimes inconsistent and arbitrary, were easy to understand. They found a receptive public and had a lasting influence.

Man-made structures too came to be admired as picturesque. 'The old town of Edinburgh', wrote Sir John Stoddart in 1800, 'abounds, perhaps more than any other in Britain, with singular and picturesque combinations'. This tourist found 'the abruptnesses and inequalities of the ground – the antiquity and peculiar style of the dwelling-houses and public buildings, some of them decaying, some deserted, some renovated – the narrow and winding streets, at one time connected by steep declivities or flights of steps, at another overlaid by transverse arches . . . well worthy the observation of the true painter.' (*Plate, p.115.*)

Watercolour drawing

The depiction of trees, clouds, rivers, harbours, lakes, fields and hills called for a medium more expressive of atmosphere than line alone, and the taste for picturesque scenery (together with the recent availability of ready-made, portable cakes of pigment) gave an impetus to the development of watercolour. Watercolour was well suited to the depiction of open-air life, of country houses in rolling, sunlit parks, of distant towns and farm buildings with figures enlivening the foregrounds.

An earlier topographical tradition had already been built up which reflected the pride of ownership and the pleasure English people took in their surroundings. It taught artists to draw buildings (*Figs 2,5*) and animals (*Fig. 8*) with complete assurance and instilled a respect for the particular and varying character of places. In the best work of the topographical watercolour artists, architecture and its landscape setting are shown, together with various human activities, as an economic and historical whole. Both these traditions lie behind the aquatints reproduced in this book.

The Industrial Revolution

In 1707 Abraham Darby, a Bristol Quaker, moved to

FIG. 10 **Liverpool from the Fort**

Drawn and engraved by John Thomas Serres

One of a set of four views of the port of Liverpool by Serres, a marine painter. Liverpool had overtaken Bristol as the greatest English port, apart from London, trading with America.

Published March 1797. 435 × 570 mm. [K.Top.18.76f]

~ 22 ~

Coalbrookdale in Shropshire where he took over a semi-derelict furnace and smelted iron, using for the first time coke instead of charcoal to reduce the ore. This enterprise was expanded by successive Abraham Darbys, and became one of the most extensive iron-works in the land. In 1767 the proprietors of Coalbrookdale first laid down iron rails for conveying ore; and about this time James Watt began the application of steam power to the traction of carriages on rails. In 1779 the first large cast-iron bridge was cast at Coalbrookdale, to span the Severn a mile or so upstream.

'With all their vast machinery, the flaming furnaces and smoking limekilns form a spectacle horribly sublime', considered one observer in 1780, recalling Milton's *Paradise Lost*, 'while the stupendous iron arch, striding over the chasm, presents to the mind an idea of that fatal bridge . . . from the boundaries of hell.' Spectacular conflagrations of other kinds had a similar appeal. (*Fig. 10, Plate, p.57.*) Mills, mines, and factories were commonly admired before their worse effects began to be felt (*Figs 8,9; Plate p.99.*) At Tintern the author of *A picturesque guide to Bath and the adjacent country* (1793) reported: 'Our contemplations were presently disturbed by the sight of a number of smelting-houses on the banks of the Wye, and much too near the Abbey: clouds of thick black smoke, and an intolerable stench, issued from these buildings, disgusting to the utmost degree and entirely destroying the landscape. Here and there we could discover a select spot that might have afforded a sketch, but we were disappointed and vexed.'

Transport and journeys

Towards the end of the eighteenth century the improvements in road-making (*Fig.11; Plate, p.53*) of Thomas Telford and John McAdam encouraged innovations in carriage design. Light, steel-sprung vehicles which rode smoothly and turned easily conveyed travellers in relative comfort, and at the right pace for observing the scenery. These improvements made possible a network of stage-coach connexions which was to reach its highest speed and efficiency just when railways were about to put them out of business (*Plates, pp.41, 125.*)

Fig. 11 **Gravel pits. A view at Hatfield, Herts.**
Drawn and engraved by J. Hassell
Hassell was a prolific draughtsman and aquatint engraver of his own and others' designs, many of which show roads and canals.
Published by F. Jukes, 1798. 300 × 385 mm. [K.Top.15.54a]

People now took to travel as an agreeable pastime rather than an unavoidable hardship. Tuition in pencil and watercolour drawing enabled them to record what they saw on tour. They wanted both previews and mementoes of places to be visited, and the trade in topographical prints expanded correspondingly. To satisfy this market, in early summer artists made their own expeditions. Their purpose was to accumulate a stock of drawings to be worked up into finished pieces for their patrons, exhibitions and publishers. (Amateur artists provided some drawings for publishers but most were made by professionals.) Time was short and the weather unpredictable. Artists had to be well-prepared. We know that Turner, for instance, using guidebooks and published engravings, made an itinerary, noting the mileage between each of the abbeys, castles, bridges, harbours and waterfalls he needed to see. Horses could be hired, but artists often walked long distances to reduce their expenses. Coastal shipping provided the quickest and cheapest transport for a London artist visiting the north or Wales, and was clearly preferable to rough roads.

William Daniell

Some artists spent a lot of time travelling. William Daniell's *A Voyage around Great Britain* (1814–25) was the result of a remarkable journey. Daniell was both an artist and an engraver, and his work, the most ambitious colour-plate book on British topography, contains in eight volumes 308 coloured aquatints engraved by him after his own drawings (*Fig.12, Plate, p.119.*) He had already completed a similar enterprise. He went out to India with his uncle Thomas in 1785 where they spent seven years making drawings, which on their return they worked up for publication in the six volumes of *Oriental Scenery* (1795–1808) sold at the high price of 200 guineas. Joseph Farington reports William Daniell's statement that 'the great facility which he had in executing aquatinta was obtained by the most severe application for seven years together . . . He said he had worked from 6 in the morning till 12 at night'.

The *Voyage around Great Britain* was prepared in

FIG. 12 **View on Puffin Island near Anglesea**

Drawn and engraved by William Daniell

Priestholm, a limestone rock about a mile long, four miles off the coast of North Wales, was once the refuge of hermits. By the nineteenth century the island was inhabited only by puffins, gulls, terns, guillemots and razor-bills. When Daniell and Ayton were taken there by boat, 'tens of thousands were wheeling and screaming in the air, and a close column of them in the sea encircled the island like a belt.'

A voyage around Great Britain, vol.II, p.31, 1815. 166 × 240 mm. [G.7043]

winters from sketches made over twelve years on summer surveys, travelling round the coast clockwise from Land's End. Daniell was joined on his first two journeys by his friend Richard Ayton who wrote lively accounts of the manners and customs of the people they met. Kirkcudbright was the limit of Ayton's collaboration and Daniell carried on both pictures and text alone. They apologise for 'frequent sailing on horse-back', when they were hindered by 'rapid tides, ground swells, insurmountable surfs, strong winds . . . no one of which could be encountered with safety in a small and open boat'.

On tour, Daniell made pencil drawings on which he wrote colour descriptions. Later he worked up sepia wash drawings to guide him in the 'biting in' of the various tone strengths of the plates. The plates were sometimes inked for single-impression printing in two or more colours. It is likely that Daniell then coloured a finished 'pull' as a guide for the colourists. They worked in greys, greens and blues, with no warmer tints. Daniell excels in suggesting weather: gathering storm clouds, the warm haze over the sea in summer, or sunlight on the roofs of a fishing village.

The Voyage around Great Britain was collected into four volumes and again the price (£60 each, 96 guineas for a large-paper copy) was high.

London

Twentieth-century visitors usually think of London as a city of history and royalty, of venerable institutions, buildings and ceremonies. Two hundred years ago, while these aspects were certainly not neglected by tourists or printmakers, for most people London's chief fascination lay in its modernity. The prodigious size and growth of London, its new architecture and engineering, the extremes of wealth and misery, of splendour and squalor attracted the admiration, awe and even fear that New York inspires today.

Thomas Malton

Thomas Malton, the son of an architectural draughtsman of the same name, drew and aquatinted in grey a dozen London views. We can compare his unsigned

FIG. 13 **Christie's Auction Room**
Watercolour drawing by T. Rowlandson for the aquatint engraving reproduced on page 59.
210 × 390 mm. Photograph by courtesy of the Trustees of the British Museum. [PD 1899–4–20–100]

water-colour of New Palace Yard – the courtyard in front of Westminster Hall – with his finished monochrome aquatint (*Figs. 2,3.*) The pale tints and elegant figures are transposed with accuracy and assurance. His *Picturesque Tour through the Cities of London and Westminster* (1792) was the first considerable collection of London prints in the medium.

Rudolph Ackermann

At the head of Malton's subscription list appears the name of 'Mr Ackermann': it was not until 1808 that Ackermann invited subscribers for his own *Microcosm of London*, perhaps the most famous of colour-plate books. We can consider its making in some detail, as the evidence happily survives. Rudolph Ackermann, born in Saxony in 1764, worked as a coachbuilder in Germany and later in Paris. He settled in London and furnished fashionable carriage-makers with his designs, some of which he published in 1791. It was Ackermann who designed Nelson's funeral car (*Fig. 16*) in 1806. He married an Englishwoman and started a drawing school

and gallery, 'The Repository of Arts' at 101 Strand (*Fig. 1*), where he also set up business as a print-seller and dealer in artist's materials. Here Ackermann published one of the earliest 'glossy magazines', which he also called *The Repository of Arts*. He became something of an arbiter of taste and the Repository of Arts a place where people were pleased to be seen passing the time of day.

Thomas Rowlandson

Around 1797 Ackermann's shop brought him into contact with the brilliant draughtsman and caricaturist Thomas Rowlandson, who had fallen on hard times. Rowlandson, who had studied at the Royal Academy and possibly in Paris, dissipated an inheritance in gambling and conviviality, which gave him an unrivalled experience of both low life and fashionable society. From then on until 1822 Rowlandson supplied hundreds of designs for Ackermann's publications, as well as making drawings that were etched and sold as individual prints (*Plate, p.43*), among them the six *Views of London* – the

FIG. 14 **Mounting guard, St James's Park**

Watercolour drawing by T. Rowlandson

On the parade-ground to the west of the Horse Guards, built 1745–48 to William Kent's design, the Changing of the Guard and inspection of the Household Cavalry take place in summer. This watercolour was produced for an aquatint by J. Bluck (*see* Fig. 15).

Photograph by courtesy of the Trustees of the British Museum. [PD 1880–11–13–2323 Crace]

'Turnpike' series of 1782 (*Plate, p.41*).

Ackermann in 1809 arranged Rowlandson's collaboration with the author William Combe in the *Tours of Dr Syntax* which satirised William Gilpin and his picturesque tours. Combe too had gambled away a fortune and was confined in the King's Bench Prison for debt. Combe wrote the text of vol. 3 of the *Microcosm* and W. H. Pyne the remainder.

Ackermann's first book, *The Loyal Volunteers* (1799) was calculated to flatter those who had worn (or paid for) the gorgeous uniforms to be seen in the plates, coloured and gilded by hand after Rowlandson's drawings. Eight years later in the *Microcosm* Ackermann exploited Rowlandson's talents more fully in populating the plates with 'lively representations of almost every variety of character that is found in this great metropolis'.

The spectacle of a city consists as much in the life of its inhabitants as in the appearance of its streets and buildings. Ackermann in his Preface suggests that, because in earlier topographical books 'the buildings and figures have almost invariably been designed by the same artists, the figures have been generally neglected, or are of a very inferior cast, and totally unconnected with the other part of the print'. To remedy this, 'attention has been paid . . . to the general air and peculiar carriage, habits, etc. of such characters as are likely to make up the majority in particular places', including, unusually, interior views.

The subjects treated in the *Microcosm* were by no means restricted to the monuments and showpieces of London but present a cross-section. Of 104 plates, 22 record public buildings and the functions of government. Courts and prisons (*Plate, p.55*) take up fifteen plates — a high proportion, when we consider that fourteen depict places of worship (including a synagogue, a Roman Catholic chapel and a Quakers' meeting) and ten show financial activities. Theatres, with ten plates, are well represented (*Plate, p.45.*) There are nine plates of charities, including schools. Learned societies get eight plates, the fine arts (*Fig.13; Plate, p.59*) five, and markets and fairs four. This leaves seven miscellaneous

FIG. 15 **Mounting guard, St James's Park**
Aquatint by J. Bluck
See Fig. 14.
The Microcosm of London, vol.II. 1808. [190.e.2]

subjects, such as 'Fire at Albion Mills', (*Plate, p.57.*) Ackermann wanted to use Rowlandson's humour and sharp observation of figures and faces in a book of London views; but the scrupulous draughtsmanship needed for the buildings may have been considered a waste of his distinctive talent. A tight schedule of monthly numbers, each with four plates to be designed, engraved, proofed and coloured, could not rely exclusively on Rowlandson's doubtful punctuality. In the event Ackermann commissioned the French emigré artist, Charles Augustus Pugin, to do the buildings and Rowlandson to supply the figures.

Charles Augustus Pugin

The *Microcosm* was Pugin's first essay in book illustration. He was employed in John Nash's office as an architectural draughtsman, where he made drawings of old buildings to serve as models for new. This training is reflected in the linear clarity of his designs (*Fig. 16*) and, as Sir John Summerson observed, 'in his feeling for subtle lighting on fine architecture'. In the margin of his

drawing for 'Covent Garden Market', though, Rowlandson wrote: 'With submission to Mr Pugin's better judgement Mr Rowlandson conceives if the light came in on the other side of ye picture the figure would be sett off to better advantage.' Rowlandson's obligation to Ackermann for employment may well have ensured his smooth cooperation with the younger and less experienced artist.

The production of the **Microcosm**

A unique and extra-illustrated copy of the *Microcosm*, Pugin's own, survives in the Art Institute of Chicago to throw some light on their partnership and procedures. It contains 24 preliminary sketches in pen and ink or watercolour by Pugin or Rowlandson; 97 detailed pencil perspective drawings for the plates by both artists together; 104 sepia and white proofs before colouring and 107 coloured impressions, some of which may have served Ackermann's colourists as models.

When both men had agreed on the view-point for a subject, Pugin would make a careful pencil drawing in perspective and in the same size as the finished plate. To this Rowlandson added his figures, usually following Pugin's directions; sometimes Pugin submitted two drawings taken from different angles for Rowlandson's consideration. A studio assistant then made a tracing of this drawing and placed it face downwards on the plate which had been laid with etching ground. He transferred the details in reverse by running both through the press. Each artist then drew his own lines on the plate with an etching needle. When the plate had been etched a proof was pulled on which Rowlandson indicated with ink washes which portions were to be aquatinted, in brown and blue. The plate was then passed to Ackermann's aquatint engravers.

In some plates Rowlandson is the more important artist. He was vitally interested in the occupations, recreations and eccentricities of his fellows and excelled where there was an emphasis on faces, action or gestures. In 'Changing guard, St James's' (*Figs 14, 15*) the frisking dogs in his drawing were evidently thought too undignified for the plate. Nor was his talent confined to figures:

in 'Christie's Auction Room' (*Fig. 13, Plate, p.59*) and in 'Exhibition Room, Somerset House' (where the Royal Academy was then housed), he sketched with equal skill the billowing bellies and jutting posteriors of the visitors, as well as the essence of each of the paintings crowded one above another on the walls.

Fifty-four *Microcosm* plates were engraved by J. Bluck and 29 by J. C. Stadler, both compatriots of Ackermann. In an edition of 1,000 there were in all 104,000 prints to be printed and coloured. The plates were printed at Ackermann's office at 101 Strand and their unvarying excellence says a great deal for his direct supervision and quality control. The prints were not all coloured at once, because they were only printed as required. Worn impressions of *Microcosm* plates occur on paper watermarked with dates as late as the 1820s but bound with the letter-press of the original edition, which was produced in one print-run.

Bringing Rowlandson and Pugin together in fruitful partnership was Ackermann's greatest single achievement. In this, the most accomplished of his colour-plate volumes, Ackermann projected an image of Regency London that has persisted, of elegant, ordered tranquillity, but with a streak of cheerful coarseness not far underneath.

Purchasers and prices

Well into the nineteenth century the wealthy and leisured classes were normally expected to have some acquaintance with architecture and gardening and with Old Master paintings and prints. Drawing was a widespread accomplishment, taught – like dancing – as a social grace, or, with a different purpose, to military and naval officers. For this discerning and well-informed public publishers of prints and colour-plate books could afford to employ the foremost artists and craftsmen, to work in a handy medium on accepted subject-matter.

The earliest sets of coloured aquatints of topographical subjects appeared in the 1790s, issued in instalments and then sold in portfolios as collections, or as illustrations (with accompanying text) to colour-plate books. It was not until 1805 that the number of colour-plate books published in a single year reached double figures, but in 1815 twenty books appeared. Between 1819 and 1825 the total was 166, with a steep decline in the number of titles after 1825.

Colour-plate books were what we would now call luxury or prestige publications. Many prints, however, were offered for sale singly, or in series of half a dozen, in particular those by local artist-engravers outside London.

The largest prints reproduced in this selection are city views (Edinburgh, Bristol, Dublin: *Plates, pp.115, 85, 127*) and the smallest is the vignette reproduced on the title-page. They have all been reduced by a quarter or thereabouts. Size was largely a matter of convenience: *Sixteen views of the Lakes* (1794–95) from drawings of John 'Warwick' Smith was advertised as 'of a proper size to bind with West's *Guide*', and indeed the book was sometimes sold with the views bound in.

This leads us to the matter of price. For larger ventures of 1,000 copies with over 100 illustrations, such as Ackermann's *Microcosm of London*, issued in three

FIG. 16 **Interment of the remains of the late Lord Viscount Nelson in the Cathedral Church of St Paul, London, 9 January 1806**

Drawn by C. A. Pugin and engraved by F. C. Lewis

Pugin made four drawings during the ceremony which were published as aquatints. Ackermann designed Nelson's funeral car: a land-ship, with bosomy figurehead, palm tree canopy and a cabin at the stern.

Published by Ackermann. 317 × 432 mm. [K.Top.23.36i]

volumes, 13 guineas a volume was the price. Daniell's publications, as we have seen, were even more expensive. Ackermann's *Oxford* (1815) and *Cambridge* (1816) were issued in monthly parts and also sold in volumes at £16 and £27 according to page-size: elephant quarto (14″×11½″) and atlas quarto (16½″×13″). Of the 1,000 copies of each issued in monthly parts from 1813 onwards the price of the first 500 was 12*s*.6*d*. and of the second 16*s*. Fielding's more modest *Picturesque tour of the English Lakes*, with 48 coloured aquatints, cost £3.13*s*.6*d*. and six guineas on large paper.

What do these sums amount to? In one of Arkwright's model factories children worked thirteen hours a day for 3*s*.6*d*. a week (2*s*.3*d*. for girls). A Leicester woolcomber in 1795 earned £47 per annum and a Manchester dyer £42. A farm labourer's wage in 1810 was 3*s*. a day in summer and 3*s*.6*d*. in 1813. Pitmen in mines about the same time made 21*s*. week and coal-hewers 30*s*. to 40*s*.

These people, however, did not buy colour-plate books. Many of the purchasers were certainly small landowners, the proprietors of estates yielding £200 to £1,000 a year. Others were in a different league. Squire Lambton, later first Earl of Durham, who reckoned that 'a man could jog along on 40,000 a year' had an annual income of £70,000. For the landed gentry of all degrees, a library, well-stocked with the right sort of books, was a prerequisite. The same was also expected of City merchants, and of lawyers, doctors and clerics. From such libraries come the colour-plate books which survive today and which we sample in this Regency album.

FIG. 17 **A view in Kew Gardens of the Alhambra and Pagoda**
Drawn by F. J. Mannskirsch and engraved by H. Schutz
Of these two follies, the pagoda remains. It was erected by Sir William Chambers in 1761–62 and inspired by his visit to China.
Published by Ackermann, 1798. 365 × 480 mm. [K.Top.40.46x]

Further reading

J. R. ABBEY: *Scenery of Great Britain and Ireland in aquatint and lithography, 1770–1860.* Privately printed: London, 1952

BERNARD ADAMS: *London illustrated 1604–1851.* Library Association, 1983

IAIN BAIN: *William Daniell's 'A Voyage round Great Britain', 1814–1825.* Bodley Head, 1966

PETER BICKNELL: 'The picturesque scenery of the Lake District. 1752–1855'. *The Book Collector.* Spring, Summer, Autumn 1987

JOHN FORD: *Ackermann 1783–1983: the business of art.* London: Ackermann, 1983

COLIN FRANKLIN: *Themes in aquatint.* San Francisco: The Book Club of California, 1978

RICHARD T. GODFREY: *Printmaking in Britain.* Oxford: Phaidon, 1978

ANTONY GRIFFITHS: *Prints and printmaking. An introduction to the history and techniques.* British Museum Publications, 1980

MARTIN HARDIE: *English coloured books, 1983* Bath: Kingsmead Reprints, 1973

The illustrated Wordsworth's Guide to the Lakes, ed. Peter Bicknell. Exeter: Webb & Bower, 1984

FRANCIS D. KLINGENDER: *Art and the Industrial Revolution:* Evelyn, Adams & Mackay, 1968

CHARLES LANE: *Sporting aquatints and their engravers.* 2 vols Lewis: Leigh-on-Sea, 1978, 79

The Microcosm of London. By T. Rowlandson and A. Pugin. Text by John Summerson. King Penguin Books, 1943

SARAH T. PRIDEAUX: *Aquatint engraving.* London: Duckworth, 1909

RONALD RUSSELL: *Guide to British topographical prints.* Newton Abbot: David & Charles, 1979

FIONA ST. AUBYN: *Ackermann's illustrated London.* Ware, Herts.: Wordsworth Editions, 1988

CARL O. SCHNIEWIND: 'A unique copy of The Microcosm of London acquired for the Charles Deering Collection', *Bulletin of the Art Institute of Chicago,* September-October 1940

ROBERT SOUTHEY: *Mr Rowlandson's England,* ed. John Steel. Woodbridge: Antique Collectors' Club, [1985]

R. V. TOOLEY: *English books with coloured plates, 1790–1860.* (Revised edition) Dawson, 1979

CARL ZIGROSSER: 'The Microcosm of London', *The Print Collector's Quarterly,* April 1937

Entrance of Tottenham Court Road Turnpike with a view of St James's chapel
Drawn by T. ROWLANDSON and engraved by H. SCHUTZ
One of six views of the entrances into London where the Turnpike Trusts collected tolls for road maintenance.
The resulting traffic jams provided an attractive subject for Rowlandson.
Views of London, No.3, published by Ackermann's Gallery, 1 April 1798. 305 × 410 mm. [K.Top.22.6.c]

THE PLATES

A bird's-eye view of Covent Garden Market, taken from the Hummums

DRAWN AND ENGRAVED BY THOMAS ROWLANDSON AND AUGUSTUS PUGIN

AQUATINTED BY J. BLUCK

Covent Garden, which takes its name from the garden of the convent or abbey of Westminster, was until 1974 the main fruit and vegetable market of London, and is still the site of the Royal Opera House.

The market began in 1656 as a few stalls in the garden of the Earl of Bedford's house, and permanent market stalls were built on the south side of Inigo Jones's piazza as early as 1705. They were rebuilt in 1748 and later, in two rows of single-storey lock-up shops with low-pitched roofs and chimneys. By the mid-eighteenth century flowers, potted shrubs and herbs were also on sale; one seedsman sold live hedgehogs as pets to keep down beetles.

Jones's church of 1650, St Paul's, is in the middle background of this view, taken from the Turkish bath-house in the south-east of the market place.

Published by R. Ackermann, January 1811. 355 × 492 mm. [K.Top.22.28.c]

Sadlers Wells Theatre

DRAWN AND ENGRAVED BY THOMAS ROWLANDSON AND AUGUSTUS PUGIN

AQUATINTED BY J. BLUCK

In 1683 a Mr Sadler, surveyor of highways, opened a place of entertainment for music and dance on the site of the Wells, a medicinal spring which had been closed down at the Reformation. During the eighteenth century acrobats, clowns, sword-dancers and tight-rope walkers performed at Sadlers Wells.

In 1802 a new management abandoned rope-dancing and tumbling, and introduced 'aquatic entertainments'. Wobbly effigies of Neptune and his horses sailing in from the wings are depicted in this print. The stage was raised mechanically to reveal a tank, the size of a swimming pool, fed from the nearby New River reservoir. Fountains, cascades and cataracts were contrived and sometimes illuminated by fireworks. In the first aquatic exhibition, of the siege of Gibraltar, model ships of the line, on a scale of one inch to a foot, floated across the stage. Some were exploded and set on fire by bombs and rockets shot from miniature brass guns.

The Microcosm of London, vol.III, no.69, R. Ackermann, 1809. 193 × 255 mm.
[190.e.3]

Buckingham House, Middlesex. A Palace of Her Majesty

DRAWN BY JOHN BURNET

AQUATINTED BY R. HAVELL

Buckingham House, built by the Duke of Buckingham *c*.1700, was sold by his son in 1762 to King George III, and in 1755 settled on Queen Charlotte for life. The king kept his vast library there, which was later presented to the British Museum by King George IV. In 1825 George IV employed John Nash to replace Buckingham House by a largely new palace in Bath stone, which nevertheless retained the shell of the earlier house and much of the plan. He did not live to see it completed, and Queen Victoria was the first monarch to live in Buckingham Palace.

This winter view was taken from the south side of the frozen canal in St James's Park.

W.H. Pyne, *A series of picturesque views of noblemen's seats*, 1815. 220 × 299 mm.
[199.i.4]

The action between the British and American frigates on the Serpentine, Hyde Park, 1 August 1814

On 1 August 1814, to celebrate both the visit of the Allied Sovereigns and the centenary of the accession of the House of Hanover, a mock sea battle was fought on the Serpentine in Hyde Park. 'The Grand Fleet . . . favoured by a spring tide . . . in the shape of a shower, had by noon floated into deep water, and formed the line', wrote an observer. 'The disproportion, however, between its strength and that of its mimic antagonists was . . . certainly not necessary to the victory of a British fleet fighting in sight of its own shores . . . The Kensington shore was lined with fireworks to cut off all retreat in that quarter'.

'First, we saw a frigate from the English fleet sailing majestically down the Serpentine, with the wind abaft the boom, to attack two ships of similar force . . . detached from the French fleet, under American colours (the stripes) . . . A smart engagement ensued, which ended by lowering the American colours.'

The frigates and their prizes were then towed up to the top of the Serpentine where the English fleet was moored and a balloon rose with the news of victory.

Published by T. Palser, 1814. 228 × 337 mm. [K.Top.6.6n]

Lambeth Chapel

DRAWN BY T. D. W. DEARN

ENGRAVED BY CHARLES ROSENBERG

Lambeth Chapel, built in 1808 at the south-west corner of Lambeth Road and Kennington Road, was destroyed during the Second World War. The designer was the Rev. William Jenkins, an itinerant preacher who also practised as an architect and surveyor. His chapels, built on a uniform plan, provided the model for others. The increase in the size and number of such chapels reflected the conversion of men of substance and zeal to an independent Methodist movement, as well as the absence of Anglican churches in recently populated areas.

Published by C. Rosenberg & T. Walser, 1812. 223 × 318 mm. [K.Top.41.1m]

View of the excavated grounds, for the Highgate-Archway, taken 1812

DRAWN BY AUGUSTUS PUGIN

ENGRAVED BY J. HILL

From 1600 onwards the main road from London to the north-west passed through Highgate village, 400 feet above sea-level. The one-in-ten gradient was tolerable for the foot traffic of man and beast, but difficult for horses drawing wagons or coaches.

In 1809 Robert Vazie, a mining engineer, suggested the construction of an 'archway' under Highgate hill, of which 360 yards would be in a tunnel and the rest in a cutting. To carry out this plan the Highgate Archway Company was set up, but on John Rennie's advice the tunnel was further reduced.

In the early hours of 13 April 1812 the tunnel collapsed because, according to the report in the *Gentleman's Magazine*, of parsimony with the bricks and cement used for lining. 'It is now wisely determined by the proprietors to reduce their tenebrious tunnel to an arch of about thirty feet in length, which will be under and will support Hornsey Lane.' As this meant a break in the old Highgate – Hornsey road, a stone viaduct sixty feet high, now Archway Road, was opened in 1813, replaced in 1877 by a cast-iron arch. Tolls were levied on all traffic until 1871.

Published by R. Ackermann, October 1813. 381 × 449 mm. [K.Top.30.1.1g]

The Pass-room at Bridewell

DRAWN AND ENGRAVED BY THOMAS ROWLANDSON AND AUGUSTUS PUGIN

AQUATINTED BY J. HILL

In the City of London the pass-room at Bridewell was the clearing house where female vagabonds from distant parts of the country were confined for seven days before being sent back to their own parishes. Bridewell, formerly a royal palace, combined a charitable foundation with a work-house and prison for men and women. 'In the cellar is a bath in which the prisoners are occasionally washed', wrote William Combe, 'but there is no yard for them to walk in, which is a great defect in any house of this description.'

Prisons and law-courts are depicted in fifteen plates of the *Microcosm of London* – only fourteen show places of worship and there are ten each of theatres and financial institutions. Sometimes the indelicacies of Rowlandson's sketches were ironed out for publication. In his drawing for this plate a weeping pregnant woman is being admitted to the female ward and a notice on the wall reads: 'Whoever dirts her bed will be punished.' In the aquatint, however, the woman's condition is not noticeable, and the inscription is illegible.

In London as many as a third of all prisoners brought before the magistrates were women, who also comprised one quarter of those committed for trial at quarter sessions and assizes. In rural areas women accounted for only one tenth of prosecutions.

The Microcosm of London, vol.I, no.12, R. Ackermann, 1808. 193 × 255 mm.
[190.e.1]

Fire at Albion Mill

DRAWN AND ENGRAVED BY THOMAS ROWLANDSON AND AUGUSTUS PUGIN

AQUATINTED BY J. BLUCK

The Albion flour-mill on the Surrey side of Blackfriars Bridge was one of the earliest all-iron plants, completed in 1769 to the design of Robert Mylne. When on 3 March 1791 a fire was discovered, the Thames was at low tide and the fire-engines, then provided by the insurance companies, were ineffective. No lives were lost but the mill and most of the flour and grain were destroyed. 'Of the peculiar facility with which property of all kinds . . . is insured against fire,' wrote William Pyne, 'foreigners can form but a very inadequate idea from any establishment of this nature in their own country.'

Each insurance company insisted that their policy holders display the company's metal wall plaque, known as a firemark, on the buildings insured. This led to confusion and needless loss of property until the companies eventually in 1833 pooled their resources in the London Fire establishment.

The Microcosm of London, vol.II, no.3, R. Ackermann, 1808. 193 × 255 mm.
[190.3.1(3.)]

Christie's auction room, 1808

DRAWN AND ENGRAVED BY AUGUSTUS PUGIN AND THOMAS ROWLANDSON

AQUATINTED BY J. BLUCK

In 1766 James Christie resigned his commission in the Royal Navy to establish himself as an auctioneer in Pall Mall, selling everything from sedan chairs to chamber pots. After the French Revolution put many works of art on the market, Christie specialized in picture sales, one of which is shown here. In 1823 Christie's son removed the auction rooms to King Street where they remain today. Rowlandson's drawing is reproduced on p.29. In the print Pugin has supplied the cornice, lantern light and fireplace, and Rowlandson's figures have been rearranged. Rowlandson sketched both the public and the pictures they were looking at. In a few strokes he condensed the essentials of each painting, and the interest which the lot under the hammer (a Venus) aroused.

The Microcosm of London, vol.I, R. Ackermann, 1808. 193 × 255 mm. [190.e.1]

A view of the first bridge at Paddington and the accommodation barge going down the Grand Junction Canal to Uxbridge

Canals dug by gangs of 'navigators', or 'navvies', linked London with the industrial Midlands. James Baker, author of *A Picturesque guide through Wales* (1795) saluted canals in cheerful doggerel:

> Resistless labour each obstruction mocks,
> Forces the mounds and cleaves the rugged rocks.
> Hail, liquid plains! By art's attraction drawn
> To scale the steep, or sweep the distant lawn.
>
> Hail, fertilizing streams! Where'er ye glide,
> Reviving Commerce woos your gentle tide.
> By you rich presents every hour are sent
> To Father Thames, to Severn or to Trent.

In 1795 land at Paddington was leased to the Grand Junction Canal Co. for extending their canal from Paddington to Brentford, where the River Brent runs into the Thames. On 1 June 1801 the Paddington Canal was opened for traffic and the first barge arrived with passengers from Uxbridge at the Paddington basin, now known as 'Little Venice'.

Anonymous. Published by Laurie & White, 1801. 285 × 430 mm. [K.Top.28.15f.]

View from Richmond Hill

DRAWN AND ENGRAVED BY RICHARD HAVELL, 1814

The famous prospect of the Thames attracted distinguished residents to Richmond Hill and visitors to the Star and Garter Inn. This view, looking west towards Twickenham, was taken from the uncultivated opening between the terrace and the Inn. On the right is Wick House, which was built in 1771 for Sir Joshua Reynolds, founding President of the Royal Academy, to a design by William Chambers, the Academy's first treasurer. 'The sloping sides of the Hill are intersected with groves, gardens and numerous finely situated residences, commanding views of the noble river, fresh green meadows, solemn woods and blue distances', wrote William Pyne, and so they still appear, nearly two centuries later.

A series of picturesque views of noblemen's seats, London, 1815. 210 × 317 mm.
[199.i.4]

Ancient Kitchen, Windsor Castle

DRAWN BY J. P. STEPHANOFF

ENGRAVED BY W. J. BENNETT, 1819

'Perhaps there is no other country where so much nice and curious attention is paid to eating and drinking, nor where the pleasures of the table are thought of such serious importance and gratified at so great an expense', wrote Robert Southey in *Letters from England by Don Manuel Alvarez Espriella* (1807).

In his host's kitchen this fictional visitor 'could not but admire the comfort and cleanliness of everything . . . the copper and tin vessels, bright and burnished, the chain in which the spit plays, bright; the plates and dishes ranged in order along the shelves. There is a back-kitchen in which all the dirty work is done . . . The order and cleanliness of everything made even this room cheerful, though underground, where light enters only from an area'.

The subterranean kitchen at Windsor Castle was rather old-fashioned. Southey's traveller goes on to describe a modern feature lacking at Windsor – the kitchen range, invented by an American, Count Rumford. In the Windsor kitchen the spits are turned by the chimney's draught.

W. H. Pyne, *History of the Royal Residences*, vol.1., 1819. 195 × 250 mm.
[60.g.11(1.)]

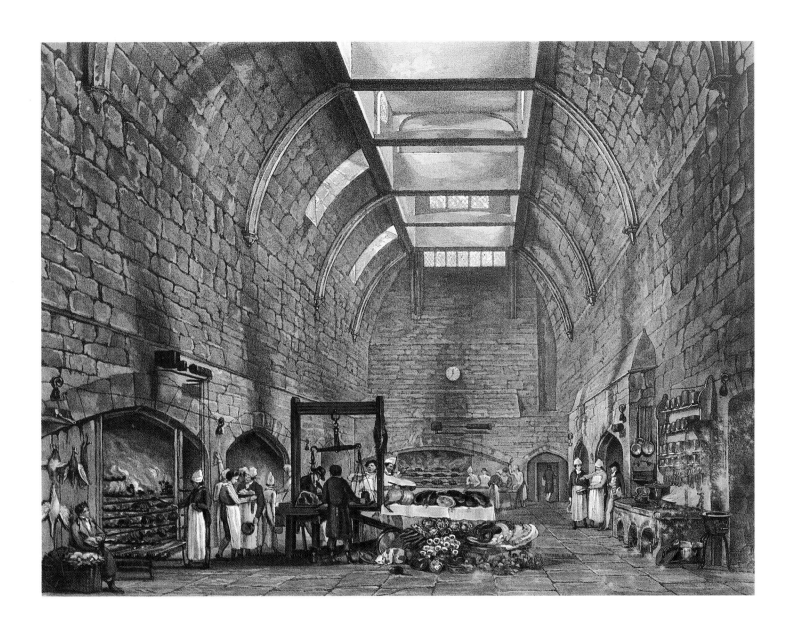

Eton School Room

DRAWN BY A. PUGIN

ENGRAVED BY J. STADLER, 1816

The older English public schools were originally religious or charitable foundations for the free education of a fixed number of children, usually called scholars. Paying pupils were also admitted. By 1800 Eton, Winchester, Westminster, Charterhouse, Harrow and Rugby, where paying pupils from all over the country formed a clear majority, already enjoyed the social prestige they have since retained. As at those grammar schools which kept their charitable and local character, the teaching at the public schools was almost exclusively literary and classical.

In this picture of the Upper School at Eton three ushers are shown conducting classes at the same time. 'None are received into the upper school, till they can make Latin verses, and have a tolerable knowledge of the Greek', explained Ackermann's *History of the Colleges*. The boys were otherwise left largely to their own devices. The Collegers or scholars lived without supervision in College in spartan conditions. The Oppidans lodged with landladies or dames, who provided breakfast, washing facilities and nursing in sickness.

A History of the Colleges, R. Ackermann, 1816. 205 × 269 mm. [732.l.27]

High Street, Oxford

DRAWN BY W. DELAMOTTE

AQUATINTED BY L. GARNAUT

Oxford in the early nineteenth century offered the visitor the great buildings of earlier centuries as yet unrestored, amid the winding walks and well-sited groves of more recent planting. Country folk still drove their flocks and herds to market over Magdalen Bridge. In this print a wagon trundles up an almost empty High Street past University College, while further on a 'crocodile' of undergraduates approaches the University church.

Most undergraduates were drawn from the nobility and landed gentry. While neither Oxford nor Cambridge then undertook professional training in medicine or law, all candidates for Holy Orders in the Church of England passed through the universities.

Outside Queen's College a disabled sailor is depicted begging alms from passers-by. He has chalked on the pavement 'Nelson – Peace'. Within eighteen months of the victory of Waterloo some 300,000 soldiers and sailors were to be discharged, most with neither pension nor medal. 'We's all in mourning here for Mr Nap' (i.e. Napoleon), the old tar told the Oxonian in *The English Spy* when he visited Portsmouth.

Published by W. Delamotte, Oxford, 1813. 513 × 707 mm. [K.Top.34,23a]

Epsom, Derby Sweepstakes, 29 June 1792

DRAWN BY J. N. SARTORIUS
ACQUATINTED BY J. W. EDY

This is one of eight racing prints engraved after J. N. Sartorius, which show 'rocking horse' contestants approaching the finishing post in the Derby. They are urged on by the spectators, some of whom are mounted – a hazard not forbidden by the Jockey Club until 1838. By current convention a good horse required a long back and tiny head; tails and ears were often cropped or docked. A French visitor described English horses as gaunt and meagre and complained that 'an awkward manner of stretching out their necks deprives them of all their beauty'. Severe training methods included sweating, purging, hard work in heavy rugs and trials over the full distance of the race.

Of 'the generality of bets which relate to the turf', William Combe explains in *The Microcosm of London*, it 'is not the custom among these noblemen and gentlemen to pay on the spot where the bets have been lost, but on the return of the respective parties to town, at Tattersall's', the foremost blood-stock auctioneers, then at Hyde Park Corner. 'Debts of this kind are settled here to an incredible amount'.

The painter Ben Marshall, who left London to set up in Newmarket, is supposed to have said, 'A man will give me fifty guineas for painting his horse who would think ten too much for painting his wife'.

Published by J. Harris, 1792. 362 × 527 mm. [K.Top.40.42.2b]

Margate from the Parade

DRAWN BY PHILIPPE J. DE LOUTHERBOURG

ENGRAVED BY J. HILL

A contemporary guide informs us that 'Margate . . . a poor, inconsiderable fishing place . . . rose at once to wealth and consequence, owing to the universal recommendation of sea air and bathing, and the rage Londoners had of spending some of their summer months on the sea coast'. Margate enjoyed an advantage over south coast resorts: 'The southerly winds which generally prevail at that season, blow off the land, which renders the sea perfectly smooth and the water clear'.

Bathing machines (there are a couple in this print) were invented by the Margate Quaker, Benjamin Beale, and enabled the bather to walk straight into the sea, concealed from public gaze by a canvas shutter. Bathers were also well catered for ashore: 'The bathing-rooms are not only well situated as to their easy access to the machines', wrote George Saville Carey (in *The Balnea*, 1801), but also provided 'a pleasant retreat, at a small subscription, where you are furnished with the news of the day, and have a pleasant look-out in the morning over the green ocean . . . Each room is generally provided with a pianoforte'.

Published by L. & W. Macgavin, October 1808. 337 × 500 mm. [K.Top.17.4e]

Dover Castle from the Beach

DRAWN BY E. DAYES

ENGRAVED BY F. JUKES

When the Dauphin of France was the ally of King John against the barons in the thirteenth century, the French king, inquiring where his son was, was told 'At Stamford'. The king replied 'What? has he not got Dover Castle? By the arm of St James, then my son has not one foot in England'.

The foundation of the keep was laid in 1153 by Henry II, with walls eighteen to twenty feet thick and an embattled summit 465 feet above sea level. During the Napoleonic wars the fortifications were repaired and extended, and cannon mounted – in addition to the brass gun twenty-four feet long, called 'Queen Elizabeth's pocket pistol', cast in 1544 and presented to her by the Dutch:

'Sponge me well, and keep me clean,
And I'll throw a ball to Calais green.'

So ran a boasting rhyme, but if this ancient 'honey-combed' gun had been fired it would surely have burst.

Published by F. Jukes, December 1810. 379 × 556 mm. [K.Top.16.–51i]

Banquetting Room, Brighton Pavilion

DRAWN BY A. PUGIN

ENGRAVED BY J. LE KEUX

The original Pavilion was designed for the Prince Regent in 1784 by Henry Holland, in the form of an oval saloon with Ionic columns outside it, and a plain wing on either flank. With John Nash's alterations this structure gradually assumed an ever more extravagantly Oriental appearance. The Pavilion cost a great deal, but once it was completed, the Prince, now King George IV, lost interest in his new toy, and visited it for the last time in March 1827.

The cornice of the Banquetting Room, inlaid with pearl and gold and adorned with pendant trefoils alternating with silver bells, is supported at the angles by golden columns, each surrounded by lances entwined by serpents. In the cupola a luxuriant and fruited plantain is depicted, from which emerges a dragon of metallic green and silver. From the claws of the dragon is suspended a magnificent lustre. This was taken down at the command of William IV, who feared that under its weight (about one ton) the supports might give way but has since been reinstated.

The nearest figure seated on the right-hand side of the table is the architect, John Nash.

J. Nash, *The Royal Pavilion at Brighton*, London, 1827, p.20. 260 × 388 mm.
[557*.h.19]

Pembroke Hall &c, from a window at Peterhouse

DRAWN BY FREDERICK MACKENZIE

ENGRAVED BY J. C. STADLER

This view of Cambridge, taken from the north side of the Fellows' Building at Peterhouse, looks down on the churchyard of Little St Mary's. To be seen on the far side of Trumpington Street are Pembroke College chapel, designed in 1663 by the young Christopher Wren, and the tower of St Botolph's church. To the east is the Saxon tower of St Benet's; and further east the tower of Great St Mary's, the University church. On the horizon King's College chapel appears in outline. It would now be obscured by the tower of the Pitt Building of the Cambridge University Press.

R. Ackermann, *A History of the University of Cambridge*, 2 vols., vol. 1, 1816.
200 × 265 mm. [127.i.10]

Holkham House, Norfolk, the seat of Thomas William Coke Esq. M.P.

DRAWN BY MISS ELIZABETH BLACKWELL

ENGRAVED BY R. HAVELL & SON, 1818

Holkham Hall was built between 1734 and 1761 to William Kent's design, in white brick dug from the estate. In order to avoid cutting the bricks, which would have caused a discoloration of their surfaces and increased the number of joints, no less than thirty moulds of different shapes and sizes were used. The grounds were laid out by 'Capability' Brown in 1762, with a large lake to the west of the house and a distant view of the sea.

The opulence of Holkham was maintained by improvements in agriculture. An observer, writing in 1816 of wheat cultivation, recalled that 'in the whole tract between Holkham and [King's] Lynn not an ear was to be seen, nor was it believed that one would grow . . . What a change has been effected by capital skill and industry!' There was scarcely a weed to be seen. 'The ground exposed on cutting the wheat was as clean as a barn floor'. Thomas Coke, later Earl of Leicester, working in a labourer's smock, taught his tenants crop rotation and in the forty years up to 1816 increased the yield of his estate nearly tenfold.

Coke's Agricultural Meetings held in July at Holkham were open to anyone interested; experiments were made and models exhibited. His annual sheep-shearing was another event of national as well as local importance.

R. Havell, *A series of picturesque views of noblemen's and gentlemen's seats*, London, 1818. 200 × 293 mm. [199.i.4]

South East view of Ely Cathedral

DRAWN BY W. ANSLOW AND ETCHED BY W. J. WHITE

AQUATINTED BY M. DUBOURG

An abbey was founded in the seventh century by St Etheldreda on the Isle of Ely, the only high ground rising out of the Fens before they were drained in the seventeenth century. The Fens were the last stronghold of Hereward the Wake in his resistance to the Normans. The abbey was rebuilt by the Normans and became a cathedral in 1109.

The tall western tower, decorated by tier upon tier of close-knit arcading, is crowned by a lantern storey, flanked by octagonal turrets. The long roof-line of the Norman nave leads to Alan of Walsingham's octagon at the crossing, an upper timber lantern, begun in 1322 and built over twelve years. This structure consisting of vertical oak beams sixty-three feet long and three feet square, is supported by invisible hammer-beams. The lantern was much altered about 1770, but entirely renewed a century later by Sir George Gilbert Scott, who reverted to the original design.

In 1986 a donation by J. Paul Getty Jnr. ensured that land adjoining the cathedral should not be built on and so this view of Ely remains unchanged.

Published in 1813 by W. H. White, London and W. Anslow, Ely. 383 × 547 mm.
[K.Top.8 69q]

Bristol

ATTRIBUTED TO S. ANSTIE

Bristol in the Middle Ages was crowded in between the rivers Avon and Frome, and here the port and manufacturers remained in the early nineteenth century. In this view ships and smoke can be glimpsed to the right of the cathedral in the middle distance. 'The smoke issuing from the brass-works, glass-houses, etc. keeps the town in an almost impenetrable obscurity', according to a contemporary guide book; but in this anonymous print the air is fresh and breezy, just right for kite-flying, which is what the boys are about to do.

The church of St George's, Brandon Hill, designed by George Smirke, now fills the foreground.

Published October 1817. 415 × 595 mm. [K.Top.37.37e]

The Orange Grove, Bath

DRAWN BY J. C. NATTES

ENGRAVED BY F. C. LEWIS

The Orange Grove near Bath Abbey was planted with rows of elm trees. The obelisk erected by 'Beau' Nash, the Master of Ceremonies, records the restoration to health in 1734 of the Prince of Orange by the drinking of Bath waters. But cures were not always complete: 'Chronic rheumatism, habitual gout, dyspepsia – from a long course of intemperate living – are disorders not to be removed by a short course of any mineral water, and many repeat their visits yearly', observed the author of *The Balnea.*

At Bath invalids and others enjoyed music, dancing, gambling and match-making. In Tobias Smollett's *Humphry Clinker* (1771) Lydia Melford writes: 'Bath is to me a new world . . . all is gaiety, good humour and diversion. The eye is continually entertained with the splendour of dress and equipage; and the ear with the sounds of coaches, chaises, chairs and other carriages'.

In 1811 an American visitor, Louis Simond, noted in his diary: 'This town looks as if it had been cast in a mould all at once, so new, so fresh, so regular. Bath is sort of great monastery inhabited by single people, particularly superannuated females. No trade, no manufactures, no occupations of any sort, except that of killing time, the most laborious of all. Half the inhabitants do nothing, the other half supplies them with nothings'.

John Claude Nattes, *Bath illustrated by a series of views*, 1806. pl.VII.
139 × 346 mm. [199.i.7]

Fonthill Abbey, Wiltshire. View from the South

DRAWN BY H. GARTINEAU FROM A SKETCH BY T. HIGHAM
ENGRAVED BY R. HAVELL & SON, 1823

William Beckford, the millionare collector, connoisseur and novelist was heir to a Jamaican sugar fortune. Despite his wealth and abilities, Beckford, dogged by scandal, retreated, first into exile and then into the seclusion of his family estate at Fonthill. Here from 1796 onwards he was engaged in the planning, decoration and furnishing of Fonthill Abbey, the greatest of 'Gothick' follies. James Wyatt was the architect of this amazing cruciform structure, on which sometimes up to 500 men were employed at a time.

The central tower eventually rose to a height of 275 feet over the lofty central octagon at the crossing but collapsed in 1800. 'The fall was tremendous and sublime', wrote Beckford, and his only regret was that he had not witnessed it. The tower was rebuilt in stone before Beckford took up residence in 1807.

Fonthill Abbey was mirrored in an artificial lake, surrounded by unfenced lawns on which tame pheasants, partridges, peacocks and waterfowl wandered. Over five hundred acres of the estate were planted with ornamental exotics and surrounded by a twelve-foot spiked wall, six miles in extent, to keep out the hunt. Though the gates were closely guarded, Beckford complained: 'The craze for seeing the Abbey grows like the tower itself.' In 1823 Beckford sold up and removed to Bath. Two years later Fonthill tower finally collapsed, destroying most of the abbey.

R. Havell, *A series of picturesque views of noblemen's and gentlemen's seats*, 1823: pl.20. 210 × 298 mm. [199.i.4]

The South Gate of Cardiff Castle in Glamorganshire

DRAWN AND AQUATINTED BY PAUL SANDBY, 1775

John Byng, on his tour of South Wales in 1787, recorded: 'Lord Mount-Steuart's bailiff attended us this evening, to show us Cardiff Castle, which has lately been repaired, adorn'd &c. by his Lordship . . . The ivy around the old tower on the keep is cut down, the sides of which are sloped, and mowed: not a tree is planted, but only some small beds of flowers; so altogether it seems to me as only calculated for (to what it is destin'd) the town bowling green'.

In the mid-nineteenth century the romantic and picturesque character of Cardiff Castle was recovered and enhanced. William Burges's restoration for the Marquess of Bute transformed it into a perfect 'fairy-tale' castle.

Paul Sandby's *Views in Wales* (1775–77) was the first important collection of aquatint views to be published in Britain.

222 × 292 mm. [K.Top.47.36c]

A view of the stone bridge across the valley at Risca in Monmouthshire, *c*.1805

DRAWN BY EDWARD PUGH

ENGRAVED BY THOMAS CARTWRIGHT

This bridge, in use before 1805, was built by the engineer John Hodgkinson; it carried the Sirhowy waggon way from the iron works at Sirhowy and Tredegar over the river Risca to Newport, a distance of twenty-four miles. The buildings on the far side of the river are the Union Copper Co. works.

Hodgkinson dedicated this plate to the Monmouthshire Canal & the Sirhowy Tram Road Co. Tramways were early railways on which trucks were drawn by horses and, on steep slopes, allowed to run downhill and then winched back up.

395 × 565 mm. [K.Top.31.15c]

Slate quarries. A view of Harlech Castle, Merionethshire

DRAWN AND ENGRAVED BY J. HASSELL

The mountains, castles and ruined abbeys of Wales held a powerful attraction for the picturesque sightseer. To English visitors, prevented by war from travel abroad, the language, legends and customs of the Welsh gave an agreeable feeling of being in a foreign land.

Of Harlech, a native Welsh traveller, Edward Pugh, wrote: 'This, once a place of importance, is now a very poor village . . . The neighbourhood is rocky and barren, scarcely affording food for sheep.' The castle, however, 'is a noble object, situated upon a rock of great elevation above the sea . . . having an area of nearly an acre, and at each angle a strong and handsome round tower'. Pugh refers to the mining of slates and with some surprise records: 'The method of conveying the slates from the beds along the narrow ridges that hang over the frightful precipices is not considered hazardous: a man conducts a four-wheeled barrow along these edges on a narrow rail-road. When a sufficient number are ready, the slates are conveyed . . . in eight or a dozen of these . . . and thus one horse will draw many tons'.

Published by F. Jukes, 1798. 215 × 323 mm. [K.Top.47.62f]

Cataract on the Llugwy

DRAWN BY PHILIPPÉ J. DE LOUTHERBOURG
ENGRAVED BY WILLIAM PICKETT

The river Llugwy, a tributary of the Conway, forms several waterfalls, among them Rhaiadr y Wenol, (the Cataract of the Swallow) near Llanrwst.

'After we had struck out on the high road, we came to a hovel, not unlike one of those . . . delineated in Cook's *Voyages*, where we found a man and his daughter who conducted us to the spot', a contemporary tourist relates. 'The noise is heard from the road, but the wood prevents a view of the fall till seen from below, . . . a mighty torrent rushing down a precipice about eighty or a hundred feet high, between two wood-covered rocks . . . Though I was forty yards distant from the fall, the spray was so great, that the paper upon which I was sketching became completely wet'.

De Loutherbourg (see p.98), who presumably kept his paper dry, considered that 'the different tints of the oak, birch and hazel, scattered around hanging from the bare rocks add greatly to the beauty of the landscape'.

Published by R. Bowyer, 1806. 231 × 314 mm. [K.Top.46.54.l.]

Iron Works, Colebrook Dale

PAINTED BY PHILIPPE J. DE LOUTHERBOURG
ENGRAVED BY WILLIAM PICKETT

At Coalbrookdale in the gorge of the River Severn in 1709 the ironmaster Abraham Darby first smelted iron ore using coke as fuel instead of charcoal. 'Here, where fuel is abundant, limestone, the proper flux for reducing the ore, everywhere at hand, and an extensive inland navigation renders the conveyance of such heavy material cheap and easy, this ore becomes the source of astonishing wealth'.

When industrial sites as well as natural scenery came to be regarded as picturesque, even sublime, Coalbrookdale, with its forges, mills, furnaces and kilns was often depicted by artists, among them the landscape and history painter, Philippe Jacques de Loutherbourg (*b.*Strasbourg 1740, *d.*1812), who also painted stage scenery and panoramas.

In his plate of the ironworks at Madeley the chimneys pouring forth red smoke are silhouetted against the glare of molten metal, and reflected in the waters of the furnace pool. In the foreground a horse and driver drawing a sledge along a track between piles of castings are caught up in a dramatic spiral with the billowing smoke.

It was unusual in colour-plate books to record the name of the colourist.

Philippe J. de Loutherbourg *The Romantic and Picturesque Scenery of England and Wales . . . Engraved by William Pickett and coloured by John Clark*, London: printed for Robert Bowyer by T. Bensley, 1805. 230 × 320 mm. [191.g.20]

A view on the Wharf near Bolton Priory

DRAWN BY T. C. HOFLAND

ENGRAVED BY R. & D. HAVELL

The Wharfe, rising on the high moors of West Yorkshire, cuts through a gorge called the Strid, then flows towards Bolton Priory, 'a widening and brawling stream between banks of surpassing loveliness and grandeur', as T. C. Hofland described it in *The British Angler's Manual* (1839).

Hofland, a drawing master and landscape artist, exhibited at the Royal Academy when he was twenty-one, and in 1810 became the second husband of the novelist Barbara Hofland. He lived for a while in a shooting-lodge formed out of the Priory gateway: 'I am well acquainted with . . . this enchanting place, which I believe to concentrate within a few miles a greater variety of rich, wild and beautiful scenery than any other place in Great Britain'.

The fishing too was good: 'The water of the Wharfe is remarkably clear and will not yield its excellent trout and grayling to a bungler . . . On one occasion when the water was too much coloured after rain for the fly, I caught a trout by spinning the minnow . . . which weighed nearly four pounds . . . I lost no time in mounting my cob and hastening home, where I first painted my fish, and the following day ate him.'

Published at Harrogate, November 1811. 293 × 400 mm. [K.Top.45.34c]

Durham from the upper part of Clay Path

DRAWN BY W. BROWN

ENGRAVED BY JUKES & SARJENT

Durham cathedral and castle were built on a rocky plateau, surrounded on three sides by the river Wear. This easily defended site was miraculously indicated to the monks who were returning with the body of St Cuthbert to Chester-le-Street after the Danish incursions of the tenth century. The saint chose not to take up his old quarters, and, through the agency of an old woman searching for her lost cow, showed the monks that this desolate spot should be his resting place.

'I perfectly recollect Durham and its imposing position above the river', wrote William Beckford in a letter of 1811. 'Its group of palace and castle buildings makes a superb effect. Its cathedral must have been sufficiently solemn and rich when all its altars were resplendent with reliquaries and lights and when St Cuthbert was the object of the most extravagant pilgrimages.'

This view by a local drawing master, taken from the north-east, shows the mediaeval Elvet bridge.

Published May 1800. 217 × 342 mm. [K.Top.12,34f]

Penwortham, with the commencement of a battue

DRAWN AND ENGRAVED BY J.T. RAWLINGS

AQUATINTED BY A. W. REEVE

'In an age when competition is a ruling passion, when the higher orders are striving for distinction in the splendour of their residences and the luxuries attached to them, it may be of service to the amateur of the trigger to discover how his endeavours may best be crowned with success', wrote Lawrence Rawstorne, a Lancashire squire.

Many landowners were obsessed by a fashion for 'battues' and vast game-bags: 'The present mode of battues cannot be conducted in good style without a heavy expenditure being incurred', wrote Rawstorne, and he cites sums of several thousand pounds a year. It is, however, 'beautiful to see so many birds in the air at one time, and those so brilliant in plumage, so elegant in form. . . . When a number of pheasants have been driven to the end of a cover, and rise at one time, making what is called a skyrocket . . . as many as three have been killed at one shot'.

Labourers whose families were hungry and saw the woods swarming with pheasants, hares and partridges could not resist the temptation to poach game, either to fill the pot or to sell to London poulterers. The magistrates, usually themselves landowners, enforced the harsh game laws with uncompromising rigour.

Lawrence Rawstorne, *Gamonia: or, the art of preserving game*, London: Rudolph Ackermann, The Eclipse Sporting Gallery, 1837. 130 × 195 mm. [C.71.f.3]

Ruins of St Mary's Abbey, York

DRAWN BY H. CAVE

ENGRAVED BY R. HAVELL

'This ruin (formerly a noble and magnificent monastery) is situated on the walls without, and on the north side of the city', explained *The York Guide* (1803). 'At the Dissolution of monasteries by Henry VIII, that Prince ordered a palace to be built out of its ruins, called the King's Manor.' A mint for coinage was built here in 1696–97 and the Manor later leased into private hands. As this print by a local artist shows, 'the present condition of this once magnificent pile of Gothic architecture is very deplorable, only a small part remaining. What greatly contributed to its destruction were grants from the Crown . . . to carry away the stone, for the reparation of other public buildings'.

The Revd Clement Cruttwell wrote of York in his *Tour* (1801): 'The present support of the city is chiefly owing to the gentry, who make it their winter residence, as there is a great plenty of provisions of all kinds to furnish an elegant table at moderate expense.'

Published by R. Cave, 1819. 307 × 430 mm. [K.Top.45.8.3d]

Entrance into Borrowdale

DRAWN BY JOHN 'WARWICK' SMITH

ENGRAVED BY MERIGOT

The Jaws of Borrowdale form the defile which separates the alluvial valley of Upper Borrowdale from Derwentwater, and were a thoroughfare for herdsmen and shepherds. In 1769, however, 'the rocks − hanging loose and nodding forwards' reminded the poet Thomas Gray of passes in the Alps, 'where guides tell you to move with speed, and say nothing, lest the agitation of the air should loosen . . . and bring down a mass that would overwhelm a caravan'.

John 'Warwick' Smith, born in Cumberland, was taught drawing there by the Revd William Gilpin's brother, and under the patronage of the Earl of Warwick, worked in Italy as a landscape draughtsman from 1776–81.

Published 1798. 245 × 385 mm. [K.Top.10.31,2a]

Keswick Lake, Cumberland

DRAWN BY THOMAS WALMSLEY
ENGRAVED BY J. JUKES & SARJENT

'After dinner we procured a guide and boat to sail upon the neighbouring lake, called Derwent-water', wrote a traveller in 1787. 'We next went upon the water, but had not the pleasure to view its mirror-like surface, which it is so famous for in bright and serene weather'. His experience is not unusual in the Lakes: 'For now the clouds hung with threat'ning rain above our heads and the bleak winds conspired to give the watery plain an unpleasing agitation'.

'The water is also of crystalline purity,' wrote William Wordsworth in his *Guide to the Lakes*, published in its first version in 1810: 'If it were not for the reflections of the mountains a delusion might be felt, by a person resting in a boat . . . that the air and the water were one.'

There is a story, probably apocryphal, of a well-meaning clergyman who, congratulating Wordsworth on the success of his *Guide*, asked him if he had written anything else.

Published by Jukes & Sarjent, 1808. 350 × 430 mm. [K.Top.10.41h]

Finckle Street near Keswick

DRAWN AND ENGRAVED BY WILLIAM GREEN

William Green, a Manchester surveyor's assistant, was encouraged to become a painter by Thomas West, the Jesuit who wrote the first guide-book to the Lakes. In 1800 he settled in Ambleside and opened shops there and at Keswick. Green was his own engraver and publisher, and his daughters helped colour his prints. Wordsworth, with whom he was on good terms, recorded on Green's epitaph in Grasmere churchyard: 'By his skill and industry as an artist he produced faithful representations of this country'. His large output of Lake District prints includes many of farm houses, cottages, halls, churches and bridges, observed with the eye of a professional surveyor.

In his *Guide to the Lakes* Wordsworth hoped that new proprietors would avoid 'unnecessary deviations from that path of simplicity and beauty along which, without design and unconsciously, their humble predecessors had moved. In this wish the author will be joined by persons . . . who by their visits . . . testify that they deem the district a sort of national property, in which every man has a right and interest who has an eye to perceive and a heart to enjoy'.

Published *c.*1810. 284 × 452 mm. [K.Top.10.54]

Edinburgh

DRAWN AND ENGRAVED BY FRANCIS J. SARJENT

An English tourist, Sir John Stoddart, in 1800 described Edinburgh thus, starting with the North Bridge, shown to the left of this print:

'This elegant bridge, which was built in 1763, is about 1200 feet in length, and crosses the North Loch at a most singular point. On the East side below you, is a great part of the Old Town which had gradually spread into the hollow . . . whilst above . . . rises Calton Hill, with its observatory, telegraph, Bridewell', i.e. the castellated women's prison designed by Robert Adam, shown in the foreground. Stoddart was too early for the Nelson Monument (1807), the thirty-metre machicolated tower which dominates the right of the print.

'No less striking is the view to the west of the bridge, where . . . the whole range of Prince's Street lies open to the eye; in the middle is the drained loch, crossed by a vast, but ugly earthen mound, behind which lies the spire of the West Kirk [St Cuthbert's], with a distant view of the country; and on the left, you have in fine perspective, the Castle, succeeded by a picturesque range of houses, which being built on the shelving edge of the rock, are necessarily lofty, narrow, irregular and divided into a vast number of storeys.' To the left of the Castle the tower of St Giles's with its hollow corona stands out above the chimneys.

Published April 1810. 402 × 600 mm. [K.Top.49.67g]

A trip up Loch Lomond

DRAWN BY W. EGERTON

ENGRAVED BY G. HUNT, 1825

As early as 1788 successful trials were held on Dalswinton Loch of a steam boat, designed by Patrick Miller and William Symington, with a double hull of tinned iron plate, and propelled by paddle-wheels.

In 1818 John Keats, on a walking tour with his friend Charles Brown, found that 'steamboats on Loch Lomond and barouches on its sides take a little from the pleasure of such romantic chaps as Brown and I'.

Day trippers travelled far to visit sites associated with the Ossian poems and Sir Walter Scott's *Lady of the Lake*. 'The company on board, some of whom have come down the Clyde from Glasgow, &c to Dumbarton (in another steamer) . . . and jogged thence . . . over a loose-stony road for five miles to Ballock Ferry and transferred on board the 'Marian', have now ploughed about twenty miles up Loch Lomond (thirty in length), been shown distant views of the Duke of Montrose's — and serenaded with an occasional air from the piper, in the McGregor tartan.'

E., M, *Airy Nothings. Drawn and written by M. E. Esq*. Pyall & Hunt, 1825.
138 × 197 mm. [C.70.g.10]

The Cathedral at Iona

DRAWN AND ENGRAVED BY WILLIAM DANIELL, 1817

After St Columba had converted the Northern Picts to Christianity in 565 he was granted the island of Iona or Columb-cill for his religious community. Columba's austere rule proscribed females, even cows, from the settlement but later inhabitants included nuns. The cathedral became the burial-place of the Lords of the Isles and of Scottish kings. In Shakespeare's *Macbeth*, the murdered Duncan is 'carried to Colme's-kill, the sacred storehouse of his ancestors and guardian of their bones'. After the Reformation Iona's monastic buildings fell into disuse and delapidation.

Richard Ayton, *A Voyage around Great Britain*, vol.III, no.84, London, 1814–25.
166 × 240 mm. [G.7044]

The Cathedral at Iona.

Mr Owen's Institution, New Lanark (Quadrille dancing)

DRAWN BY M. EGERTON
ENGRAVED BY G. HUNT

David Dale, in partnership with Robert Arkwright, inventor of the cotton spinning frame, established a factory to exploit the water power of the Clyde. They provided not only housing for their workers but employment for destitute children.

In 1799 the Welsh cotton spinner Robert Owen married Dale's daughter and took over the mills of New Lanark. In 1809 he built the Nursery Buildings for 300 apprentices, and in 1817 a school. Children aged from one to ten were taught from a 'rational approach', by kindness, not punishments. Their singing and dancing made New Lanark something of a tourist attraction. One visitor wrote in her diary in 1823: 'Saw them dancing, very pretty but a great pity to put quadrille notions in their little heads; they also dance country dances and reels extremely well – queer dress, no shoes nor stockings, a kind of thin petticoat up to their knees on both girls and boys . . . this made of white cotton material trimmed with blue or red so that they look just like opera dancers.'

E., M., *Airy Nothings. Drawn and written by M. E. Esq.* Pyall G. Hunt, 1825.
130 × 215 mm. [C.70.g.10]

Dargle, Co. of Wicklow. A romantic glen forming part of Powerscourt demesne

DRAWN BY T. SAUTELL ROBERTS
ENGRAVED BY SUTHERLAND

The river Dargle forms a waterfall 350 feet high in Powerscourt Park before flowing in a narrow channel through a deep valley, flanked and overhung by oak woods and rocky outcrops. Only ten miles from Dublin, Powerscourt and the Dargle have attracted tourists since the mid-eighteenth century, including George IV on his state visit to Ireland. Luckily he did not go to see the waterfall, where a sluice gate had been installed to augment the flow of water. When the sluice was opened the bridge erected for the royal party was swept away.

Published June 1803. 398 × 547 mm. [K.Top.55.45a]

From Blackrook, looking across Dublin Bay towards Williamstown and Merrion

DRAWN BY ANDREW NICHOL

ENGRAVED BY JOHN HARRIS

The Dublin and Kingstown railway, the first in Ireland, was authorised by 1831 and locomotives built by G. Forrester of Liverpool ran on its six miles of track. 'With a total exemption from the expense, impurity and physical dangers of tunnels, yet without much objectionable invasion of private property . . . it opens a coast of the finest bathing strands in Ireland', wrote John D'Alton, in *The history of Drogheda*, 1844. Steam power was not the only means of traction. On a short extension to Dalkey, built in 1844, atmospheric pressure was used for the first time in the British Isles, with apparent success until 1854. Elsewhere atmospheric railways were not in use for long, usually because the leather valves that sealed the vacuum were eaten by mice.

A. Nichol, *Dublin & Kingstown railway*, Dublin: Wakeman; London: Ackermann, (etc) 1834. 250 × 300 mm. [562*.e.5]

College Green, Dublin

DRAWN BY T. S. ROBERTS

ENGRAVED BY R. HAVELL & SON

The Bank of Ireland, formerly the Parliament House, occupies the right of this view taken from Trinity College; Daly's club house and an equestrian statue of William III are beyond and to the left.

The Irish Parliament, built 1729–85 for the vast sum of £95,000, was intended to outshine Westminster. In 1785 the architect James Gandon added a portico of six Corinthian columns to the Ionic building as an entrance to the House of Lords (not visible in this view). He thought that this variety would be pleasing, but others found it discordant. When the workmen were placing the capitals a passer-by asked, 'What order is that?' Gandon replied that it was a very substantial order, that of the House of Lords.

After the Union of 1802 Irish members of parliament took their seats at Westminster and the building was purchased by the Governors of the Bank.

Published in Dublin by James del Vechio, 1816. 428 × 603 mm. [K.Top.53.20a.2]